Where Do My Words Go?

POEMS ABOUT THINGS I HOPE ARE TRUE

Bryant Burroughs

LBB Press

To Ruth

*Living a lifetime with my Heart's Desire
is a fairy tale come true*

CONTENTS

FOREWORD

There are things that ordinary language cannot convey, observed Christian Wiman, my unmet mentor who has helped me find a space of comfort at the edges of hope and faith.

Ordinary language and words rarely fail us in making sense of life, yet often prove inadequate in describing the very things most dear to us, those things that well up from beauty and love, wonder and hope.

For me, poetry is a higher language by which we employ words and creative imagination to give solidity to that which we sense, but cannot fully describe. For that reason, the sub-title of this small book of poems is "Poems About Things I Hope Are True." Things about love, life, death, hope, faith, God.

More importantly, for me poetry is prayer, perhaps even faith. I feel God most near when I'm writing poetry.

There is an intimate relationship between a poem and its creator, an intimacy into which the reader is granted access. Each of these poems has its own birth story, sometimes despite or against the wishes of its creator. In the end, each poem insisted that it come alive in its preferred way and form. Now each poem continues its life in you, the reader.

WHERE DO MY WORDS GO?

I once asked my words,
"Where do you go after I've breathed you into air?"
My words answered,
"We who are born in love and care
fly to her heart and are welcomed there."

"Though mere words, she *feels* us
and we sing ourselves to her heart:
I love you,
    I'm sorry,
        Let me help you,
            Forgive me,
                Thank you,
                    Good night,
                        I'll do that for you.

As we sing, she weaves us into a cloth of Heaven,
a cloth that ever grows.
And she sings back to us:
'Two halves now whole,
Two lives, one heart,
never again apart.'
And we mere words are blessed
to hear the song she attests."

Then I asked my words,
"What of those that are mean,
and hurt the very one I adore?"
My words answered,
"She who has loved you since nineteen
knows you're good at your very core.
Few mean words make it into her clean
heart and, ashamed and poor,
for words are not made to harm,
soon are entranced by her charm
and are changed, joining our song.
And our song grows ever on."

HYMN OF THE ABYSS ❧

The abyss looms near,
its rim more sensed than seen,
yet there, pulling and beckoning,
so near now that I can hear
its hymn of peace and fear.
Am I moving toward it
or is it moving toward me?

All of us, every one, will disappear
over its edge, bringing an end to all sorrows
and songs and sighs, a Great Reckoning.
A few friends have already vanished.
My turn will come, perhaps tomorrow
or next year or next decade,
likely sooner than I wish, and afraid.

The abyss takes all over its rim.
Into what? Do we fall ten thousand years
without time, without light,
into nothingness? Or perhaps it steers
us into Everything, and we'll laugh
to become stars and rain and birds in flight.

When I hope,
I hope that the Abyss is Dante's wall of flame that burns us clean.
Or Lewis' pleasant land in which Ghosts become free.
Or Tolkien's kind treatment in which Niggle finds his Tree.
Or Mary Oliver's scalding light scrubbing and scouring us.
And I hope that Light will embrace Darkness,
envelop it, and make it good,
so that we and Darkness find our being in Light.
And all will be well.

WHERE ON GOD'S GREEN EARTH ❧

Following Augustine, who described his soul as a house so cramped that
God could barely squeeze in

Where on God's Green Earth
can I find peace?
Fair it was when God spoke it alive,
green and good,
a poem of God
picturing that which cannot be seen.
Its seas and lands at peace,
its birds learning to sing
and lift their wings in love,
trusting the air in hope.
A man and a woman
in a pleasant garden
learning to be a pair,
the start of it all.
How else could it be but good?

My peace has leaked away,
pried from my clutch
by anxieties old and new,
angsts that disquiet and dispirit,
and cram worry into every crevice.
O Augustine, I, too, am a cramped soul.

God's Green Earth speaks into my confines:
"We are the glimmerings of the Marvelous.
        Listen to us!"
The stars sing: "We are the flares of God,
        long-watching and long-wandering,
        our very light praising the Maker."

"Run to him," say the sea's waves.
"Rejoice!" the birds sing. "Let our music gather in you."
The rivers speak softly: "All are led to the Sea, where all will be well."

All God's Green Earth sings together:
       "Draw in our music.
       Look to the Marvelous
       who holds all things.
       Seek that.
       Hold on to that."

WOULD YOU VOUCH FOR ME? ✏

Would you vouch for me
on that day all must stand
and give account for help and harm?
Would you speak for me
and make my plea?
For your love charmed me
into becoming a better man,
a better self only you perceived.
You told me my real name
and you believed
it was me.

Would you tell the gate-angel
that my heart is good
and that a good heart
is the father of good deeds,
however lived out imperfectly?
Would you say that you counted on me,
whether we faced dread or good,
each better together, not apart?

If you would so attest,
the angels would hear in thrall,
dancing at such love,
and then, at your behest,
open the gates to the Blessed
Land where we, no longer oppressed
by choice, fear, or harm,
live forever arm in arm.

SONG OF THE GATES ❧

"The whole life of the good Christian is holy desire"
Augustine – Homily on the First Letter of John

We are the twelve gates,
each a single pearl,
unbarred and unshut,
endlessly open wide
so that all may enter.

Here it is forever the Eighth Day,
illuminated by God himself,
for where God is, light must be,
and the darkness of hurt and fear
and tears are wiped away.

    Sing, ye streets of glassy gold.
    Sing, ye walls of precious stone.
    Sing, ye who enter and live.
    Sing to our bedazzling God.

We sing to you, Three-in-One,
who on the First Day
ignited light into the void.

We sing to you, Torch of God,
God-Come-Near,
who stepped across existence,
welcomed by poor shepherds
and travelers from afar,
a common manger and
a woman who said yes to an angel.
You enkindled dark lands with light
to save the Lord's Delight.

Come all who walk the highway of God.
Come all who drink the water of life.
Come all who buy food without coins.
Enjoy forever the light of God's City.

MY MOTHER CAME TO ME ⟋

My mother came to me
as I washed dishes. She visits
once in a while, as if in her land
a day is a thousand of mine,
a land somewhere other than here.
Perhaps she is accessible every day,
if I could but see.

Soaked by her presence, and I
with hands in soapy water,
called to her as warm love
suffused bones and heart and soul,
as if once again I was utterly safe,
and angst and fear and worry
fled far away.

Why does she visit, I wonder?
Perhaps to say good night
as in long ago days
her voice floated from her room
to us children:
"This has been a good day.
Rest now.
You are safe.
A good day will follow this good night."

THE LITTLE TABLE

The little table on our sun porch
is older than I am -
bought by my parents when they married.
I like to imagine it was the day
they took pictures of themselves,
just the two of them in the countryside,
as if the only people in the world.
Their images are monochromatic reminders
that they were Martha and Leland
before they were Mother and Dad.
Weeks from their wedding, their faces
are full of love and hope and a surety
that life together would be good.
My mother was a year out of marching
as a majorette in high school,
and happily unaware that she was only three years away
from her own mother's death.
My father was three years out from the Pacific war,
confident that he could bend the future to his will
as surely as gravity bends light.
I joined them a year and a week into their marriage,
their first born, a son who bore my dad's name.

There's a presence now with this little drop-leaf table
that shared time and space with them,
cozy and close with its leaves down
and, with leaves up, spacious for the family
that grew from two to six.
I wonder: does the little table talk
to the table in the hallway,
the one that was in my grandparents' house?

Oh, the stories they could tell.

WHAT HAPPENED TO LAZARUS ❧

Inspired by the silence of John 11 & 12

The badgering began as soon
as he tottered out of the tomb,
and friends and strangers
swarmed him with questions:
What did you see?
Did you see your mother and my mother?
They were such friends.
Could you hear our laments for you?
Were you afraid?
Does it hurt to be dead?
They combed through his tomb,
finding only the smell of decay,
so they backed away
and thronged around his house,
disinterested in him,
interested in knowing the unknowable.

"I'm the only one they know who once was dead",
he calmed his sisters, who kept touching him
as if he were unreal,
a dream to hold close
lest it vanish again.
His only memory was a dreamless sleep
that leaves the sleeper rested
but wobbly when awakened.
But how could he remember a sleep without dreams?

There came a dinner party,
a ruse to which Lazarus
and his Raiser were guests.
Surely, now, his hosts thought,
we will have answers.
We must have answers.
And Martha cooked and served,
and Mary wept and washed
Jesus feet with costly cream,
and dried them with her hair.
In the shocked silence, Lazarus said,
"It was like that."

DEATH IS A GARDENER

I've heard grim tales of a Reaper
who waits at the end of the field,
black-robed and staring,
sharp scythe unconcealed,
to reap the field of my years.
Not one of us escapes.

Now the edge of my field appears
but a short walk away.
People I love disappear,
some unsteady, most in fear,
all surprised to reach so soon
their field's far frontier.

"A good death is a treasure none is too poor to buy,"
said the long-dead creator of Narnia.
Please, God, I pray,
may I make a good death,
come what may,
constant through the end
to the hope that you've converted
the Last Enemy into a gardener.

JOSEPH'S SONG TO MARY

Stanza 1 Love
I thought I would live poor and hoary
in body and soul, a shaper of wood,
but you drew me into your story
of courage and motherhood,
and a God who trusted you and me
with the Child who is more than a Child.
How could this be? You and me,
the ones on whom God has smiled.
Forgive me for listening to my fears.
I shouldn't have needed an angel - only your tears.

Stanza 2 Birth
You didn't need me to bear this Child,
this newborn, this babe, God in disguise.
But I wouldn't have known a God so sure
as to use you and me to reprise
his beloved creation. For this One in our arms,
the star shines and angels sing,
shepherds roam and kings sense alarm,
for he is Morningstar with healing in his wings,
a Babe who in time will create
an endless stream at heaven's wide gate.

Stanza 3 Death
Day on day you've loved me,
but now I've run out of days.
The Hall of Souls awaits me,
beyond your touch, your arms, your gaze.
In life you've followed wherever I've gone
but now I go where none can see.
Your comfort is our Son, boon of the undone,
who gave himself as guaranty.
Our Son will save you and me
for he is Keeper of the Key.

SONG OF THE STAR

The One who is Light
made me to shine this night.
"Beam!" he declared, "It's time."
I sing as I shine, calling
to near and far: "Come!"

Come you from the East,
follow me to the One
worthy of being sought,
for he is the Way.
Come, walk this lighted way
and welcome with your gifts
the Treasure of Nations.

Come shepherds, night-watchers,
the fullness of time has come.
Come and see the marvel:
a virgin bearing a son,
a babe both God and man.
Look with awe
upon God with us.

Come, hierarchy of angels,
sing the Good News
that God has come near.
Unbidden, yet desired.
Unexpected, yet hoped for.
Look with wonder
upon the Wonder of God.

Come, Herod, even you, come.
Is your soul not worth a crown,
which is lost to rust or death?
Cast it down and bend your knees
to the One True King.

Come, all who dwell in darkness:
Bethlehem, City of David,
in you is born the Key of David
who fits the locks of souls.
Galilee beyond the Jordan,
darkness has scraped you tender.
He is coming, he is coming,
with healing in his wings.

SONG OF THE MANGER

Rest now, little babe,
you've come a long way to be
in this place on this night.
Even your father
has closed his eyes,
weary from worry,
dreaming of joys ahead
as you run and play
and learn to shape wood
into good things for life.

The one who said yes to the angel
and birthed you into my straw,
has counted fingers and toes
and kissed your eyes and nose,
and marveled at you,
infant yet infinite,
baby yet boundless,
hours old yet Maker of Days.
As you've nestled at her breast,
she's asked, "How could God's Son
come to life inside me?"
Even she can't grasp your intrusion
into the world you made,
as if an artist sketched himself
into his finest landscape.

Eons ago, you made me in the rock
that runs deep beneath us.
Now you, the Wondrous Intruder,
chose a trough for a birthplace,
hard stone smoothed by animals,
nondescript, common, unclean.
As the moon thanks the sun for its light,
now I sing back to you
my thanks and wonder.

Blessing us with your gaze,
you close your infant eyes,
and I give silent praise
for God's wondrous Surprise.

THE WORD SPEAKS

You've heard that God is far away.
    But I say
I am God-Come-Near,
water overbrimming your souls,
light overwhelming your dark,
love overcoming your fear.
Cling to me, come what may.

You've heard that God is to be feared.
    But I say
I am the shepherd who knows your name,
guards you at night in the pen
and as you graze in the meadow,
as if lion and wolf are tame.
Cast your hope on me, come what may.

You've heard that my Way is hard.
But I say
I am the Way - both path and pioneer.
My Way is for the lame,
those who cannot walk far or fast,
and the one who wanders finds no shame.
Follow me, come what may.

SONG OF THE WATER-POTS ✣

John 2 Jesus said to the servants, "Fill the jars with water,"
and they filled them to the brim. Then he told them,
"Now draw some from them and take it to the headwaiter,"

We are more ancient than our captors
who stole us from rocks older than stars.
We who were formed on the Third Day,
lorded over by Sixth Day creatures.
They chipped and shaped us into jars,
water-pots to wash filthy hands and feet.
We, shamed by their dirt and grime,
long for the mountains that birthed us.
Only the mountains know we're weeping.
Only the mountains see our true nature.

His mother asked his help, and he smiled.
Mother, here? It's only a wedding.
Mother, now? It's not time – you know that.
Mother, is it that important to you?
And she smiled.
She could have asked anything
and he would have given it.
We gasped as water fresh from the well –
cold, clear, clean -
streamed into our grimy swill,
like a fierce wind whipping through trees
without disturbing their leaves.
And we teemed anew
as on the Third Day.

Let the wedding guests rejoice!
Let the mountains rejoice!
Let the pots give voice to joy!

THE WIDOW'S PSALM ❧

*A prayer of the Widow of Nain (Gospel of Luke, chapter 7)
as she walked beside the bier of her only son.*

How long, how long must we kneel
and cry to you, until our appeal
is heard and you are stirred?
Do the ears of God hear no sound?
Are the hands of God bound?
Are the eyes of God blurred?

I had heard that you are Heaven's Breath
blowing into us a life that stops death.
Yet here am I, bereft of all save sorrow.
You, son of a widow and the Spy
of God, you didn't even try.
Does your mother have a son I may borrow?

God's only Son, why is my only son here
on this dreadful God-forsaken bier?
This son of unquenchable tears.
For no good have I wailed,
and I wonder: who else have you failed?
I'm left with sorrow to fill my years.

YOUNGEST DAY

Each day that came before
has become a yesterday.
Its skies awakened with hope,
then the sun moved and stars played,
and the day faded away,
lost in our three-score-and-ten scope,
wherein two millennia of days blink past.
We survive all our days but our last.
Then we, too, fade away
to await the Youngest Day.

The Youngest Day
will neither age nor wane.
Our false king, imperial
Time, long our master and bane,
will be unnoticed, immaterial,
as on Christmas Day with family all around,
or holding hands walking in the rain,
or a fresh dawn with birdsong its only sound.
And Time, with death and tears in train,
will be exiled to a shore far away.
And we, awakened and washed clean,
will be undefiled on the Youngest Day.

SONG OF THREE RINGS

I am the ring of love's first days,
a golden pledge
of love and help throughout life's ways,
though they could see only the edge
of the path. Their love was ablaze
as brightly as the radiant stone
that burnished her finger and captured their gaze,
as a glittering flower of love's seeds they'd sown.
    "I rejoice and sing
        that she would ask to wear me
        until the end of days
        as her Engagement Ring."

I am the ring of December,
a golden vow
whose permanence helps them remember,
in years coming after this longed-for Now,
they are to be faithful and hopeful as bride
and groom, now husband and wife –
miraculous words! – love having opened wide
the fortune of a helper and companion and guide for life.
    "I rejoice and sing
        that she would ask to wear me
        until the end of days
        as her Wedding Ring."

I, too, am the ring of that December day,
a golden band
to make the heart visible, love's display.
On that day, with ring and hand
they gave each other their consent
to never again be alone.
Instead, to be for each other a Christmas present
and put the other's help above their own.
    "I rejoice and sing
    that he would ask to wear me
    until the end of days
    as his Wedding Ring."

MAGIC TIME

The Harvest Moon at Hallows Eve
heralds the magic time – we believe –
that Advent, Wedding and Christmas weave
        in our two hearts.

We begin each year with hope yet come to such tears,
weary of life, weary of hurt, weary of fears
in our souls – the magic time soothes and cheers
        our two hearts.

We rejoice together, for we each have a whole claim
on the other – sharing a life, sharing a heart, sharing a name.
We fill each other's empty spaces with love, and so reclaim
        our two hearts.

Today magic time sings, "Come away, come away,
to a Magic Time Forever and a Day,"
in which Advent, Wedding and Christmas stay
        in our two hearts.

ALL THINGS SING A SONG

All things sing a song
known only to them.
We would join with joy
if only we knew the hymn.

There is, too, a melody
in the synchronous beat
of two paired hearts,
broken open, given away, yet complete.

I've come this long way
knowing only the one song
that you've taught me,
a mysterious plainsong.
At my best and at your behest
I sing it each day.

WHAT MUST HAVE BEEN YOUR WORDS

what must have been your words
to tell the Father your wish
to come to earth to save
those thrown upon the waves.

Did he know that your heart
would take you to a disaffected
place, to give hearts a new start?
You, the One Hoped For but unexpected,
You, the One Looked For but unwanted,
You, God on sabbatical, Creator yet creature.
Many of the disaffected and hopeless responded,
and gained your good mercy and pleasure.

Did he know that you would be
the Hands-On God who touched a leper's face
in careless indifference to disgrace?
The God on Bended Knee
who stooped to a woman cast at his feet?
The Dazzler who wanted no acclaim,
only to heal and hold and love and claim
us, your very heartbeat.

Did he ask, "Are you sure?"
And you said "Yes,
I want to endure
all their pain.
I want to cure
all their ill.
I want to secure
all their souls.
I want to detour
through death for them."

what must have been your words
to tell the Father your wish
to come to earth to save
those thrown upon the waves.

PRAYER FOR GB

Jesus,
You said,
      we are never outside your attention.
You said,
      you never lose track of us.
You said,
      you love the helpless and hopeless.
My friend GB needs help and hope.

He is like the woman who suffered
terribly a dozen awful years,
bleeding doctors all her money,
yet her malady worsened.
All she wanted,
      her only hope,
was to touch the barest edge of your clothes,
the hem that dragged in the dirt.
One day as you made your way
to heal a dying little girl,
you walked near the woman,
and she stretched out her fingers
and touched the fringe of your cloak,
and was cured.

If I asked you, would you walk near GB?
Would you send your Spirit
or one of your legions of angels
to help him touch your cloak?
He's waiting with
      arms and hands and fingers outstretched,
hoping to touch your cloak.
Please, walk by GB.

THE WRINGING OF GOD

Faith's language is filled with faded words,
depleted by repetition.
A word such as "sin",
three little letters, yet I'm called
to flee, fight, resist, confess it.
I've lost my way with it.
Sin seems like an ogre in a wood
that bolts out and bites me,
its sting causing me to lust
or worry about money, future, death,
so I think: sin isn't in *me*.
It's the infection of the ogre's bite.

Then, like Dante, I come to myself.
I *feel* sin.
Sin is my soul hurting another soul.
Sin is treating unkindly the kindest person I know,
my Heart's Desire.
Sin is being impatient with her, this one
who has trusted me with her vulnerable places.
Sin is pulling away from her, my Safe Place,
who renews our vows each night
with a touch and soft words.

There must be a reckoning, then,
a wringing out of my selfishness,
an untangling of soul and sin,
a cauterizing of cuts and wounds,
self-inflicted by fear, anger,
contempt and impatience.
A wringing by God
through his vast mercy.
For in Paradise
there is no word for sin.

WHAT ODYSSEUS HEARD

My grace is enough; it's all you need.
My strength comes into its own in your weakness.
2 Corinthians 12:9 The Message

When Odysseus the War-Hero
turned his good ship and crew toward home –
his lust sated with Calypso and Circe,
his bloodlust sated at Troy –
he yearned for Penelope and their
marriage bed made of a single tree.

Yet as he sailed past the Sirens' isle,
he listened to their singing,
though their songs offered
nothing he needed
and would wreck him on the shoals.
His faithful wife waited at home,
still he listened.
I long to be wholehearted,
to hear Jesus' words and act upon them,
for humility to sweep away pride
and serenity to quell anxieties.
Yet my progress is incremental,
Step, step, stumble, shame.
I'm impeded like Odysseus
by beautiful false offerings;
not the allures of Sirens,
but the seductive lures
of convenience, security, detachment.

What hope is there,
if that which I most want is ungraspable?
"Cast yourself upon me," whispers the One
who calls himself the Good Shepherd,
the Shepherd who is deeply glad to seek
his resistant, distracted, confused sheep —
every single one, every time.
The Shepherd of Mercy
who rejoices as he rescues.
And I rejoice in his vast mercy.

LAND, TAKE YOUR REST

Land, take your rest.
We belonged to you long before we met you.
You gave yourself to us,
to the love and laughter of children
running and playing all over you.
You nurtured the garden and apple trees,
the fig tree and muscadine vine – and their bees.
You held our house in your hand
and gave your soft earth for our pets' shrine.
We didn't know these were gifts from you,
this place upon which we could stand.

You, the most permanent among us,
could have lorded it over us,
we whose life span is measured in scores.
Instead, you tended us,
you gave our bare feet acres
filled with adventures to explore.
Soft grass became a baseball field,
a vine patch a hiding place,
a tool shed a fort,
a tall tree a ship's crow's nest.
Did our lives make you happy, Land?
Did you rejoice as we ran
across you, happy and blessed ?

Now the voices are gone,
the house and shed are gone,
and you are alone.
But I learned from you, Land,
that nothing is ever lost,
and that you keep safe our laughter and love,
playing it back for the grass and trees
and shrubs and graves and bees,
telling them, "This we will see again."
Take your rest, Land.

MARY COUNTED HIS FINGERS AND TOES

When the Universe-Maker came as a babe
into the very world he had made,
his mother counted his fingers and toes,
kissing each one, and said,
"He's perfect!"
Fingers that had flicked stars to life
and toes that had stepped across light.
Infinite winding into finite,
this babe who was God's Delight.

When the Universe-Crosser came to his own,
he chose a tiny womb
and a birth into a lowly trough
fit only for animal feed,
as if he were an odd aside.
And Mary kissed his eyes,
eyes that had seen the universe arise.
This babe who had sown
wombs, animals and seed
and made stars, moon and skies,
a God we could see with our own eyes.

SAY A PRAYER FOR THE FAITHLESS ⌇

Say a prayer for the faithless
and never wonder why.
Say a prayer for the faithless,
for we all shall die.

Say a prayer for the hopeless
who look down and sigh.
Say a prayer for the hopeless,
for hope none can buy.

Say a prayer for the homeless
for our God is nearby.
Say a prayer for the homeless,
for to him we cry.

WHAT PETER'S FEET REMEMBERED ❧

Through the rest of their days
and unto Paradise,
        Peter's feet remembered
as if only a moment before,
the feel of the sea
as he stepped atop it,
surprised to find solidity.

        And the ears of Jairus' daughter,
awash in scoffers' wails,
recalled the Healer's appeal:
"Little girl, I say to you, get up."
Whether command or plea,
like Lazarus and the Widow's son,
she stood up.

        And the hands of the woman
who touched his cloak,
the barest of touch
with the last of hope,
recalled the force of wholeness
sweeping away
twelve years of pain.

        And Thomas' finger
as he shakily probed the wound,
recalled an absence of faith
even of the tiniest mustard seed,
but, too, that the hole in Thomas' soul
had been probed and healed,
and he cried out.

        And Mary Magdalen's eyes,
now long dimmed by death,
burned with the image of the Gardener,
fresh from death and tomb,
walking in a garden of new life
and drying her tears with her name.

Though their bodies have gone to dust
in the long sleep,
I hear their witness and trust
the Shepherd my soul to keep.

PEARLS OF IGNATIUS

"I carry my chains for Christ, which are to me spiritual pearls, more prized than all the treasures of the world."

Ignatius, as he walked from Antioch to Rome to be martyred. He walked in chains and surrounded by Roman soldiers.

> My chains are my pearls,
> as I hasten to Rome like a bride
> stepping from her father's house
> to her bridegroom's side.
> Pearl-adorned, I trek toward one
> who thinks himself divine,
> and stamps his coins with pride:
> "the divine Trajan",
> conceit upon conceit.
>
> Choose! he roared at me:
> Deny and you will live.
> Hold fast and you will die.
> My lions will silence you.
>
> But will I not surely die
> whether I hold fast or deny?
> How, then, could I betray
> the One who also chose this Way?
>
> Devour me, you lions!
> Roar over my flesh and bones.
> I am the wheat of God
> sifted for his Bread!

WORDS ARE NOT FREE ❧

1

Angel, Angel, what have I done,
to be given this awful load?
To choose dumb or dumb, slow thoughts or slow words,
while in my mind they leaped and flowed.
I was told "you're so smart", but I knew otherwise.
There is no free speech because words are not free
and the cost is too much for me.

2

Angel, Angel, why do the sirens cry
"Do this and your words will flow"?
Though breathed with hope, it's a lie.
They lied: "It's something he'll outgrow."
They lied: "If he would just put it out of his head."
As if it could be cast off like a shell
or disenthralled by a spell.
And as if such a deal had not been pled.
Finally, they lied: "His father has pushed him too hard."
How, then, did it outlast my parents' tears?
They, too, suffered in silence, my encouragers and guard.
My demon has become my daemon,
as much myself as my Self, and whispering only fears.

3

Angel, Angel, was this the only way,
to hurt me so terribly?
Is the One you serve so unfair
that "for your own good" means to hurt unbearably?
I could have been like Merton
for whom the monastery's silence was solace.
Or the man in Mark 7 who could neither speak nor hear.
But is Mark 7 only another lie, or at most a promise
that some, but not all, find the way? Perhaps
I'm more like Pascal, genius reduced to scraps.

4

Angel, Angel, why does the silence
from the borders of heaven speak
more clearly than I?
Is there something in me that is too weak
to win and never fall back again?
If so, I'll not find the place I seek
along this hard way.
There is no free speech because words are not free
and the cost is too much for me.

PEARL

There is a medieval English poem
of a man who lost his dear Pearl,
and dreamed of an isle across a swift river,
and on its shore stood his treasured girl.

You claimed our hearts at your birth,
our unanticipated but oh so welcomed little girl.
Our hearts belong to you forever,
our treasure, our girl, our Pearl.

Perhaps a hard-shelled mollusk can feel pride
as it opens, after twenty years, to free its Pearl.
Surely it opens joyfully, its purpose complete,
to grow and protect and then free its Pearl.

The Pearl becomes what it was meant to be,
as a star is made to light the night
and a tree is made to stand.
A Pearl clothes love in lustrous white.

Perhaps the Pearl will live in a ring
that graces a women's hand
or on a strand that adorns her throat,
a white treasure from a grain of sand.

And there the Pearl rewards forever,
in its exquisite white-orbed reflection
that evokes love between two hearts,
the hard-shelled mollusk's affection.

A LONG WALK TOWARD GOD

Creator of the stars at night, your people's everlasting light
St. Ambrose

Come, you three, follow me
to a space you do not know.
A child conceived with no man,
God sparking himself in her womb.
Angels sing and shepherds run
to marvel at this child.
You three, hurry, come and marvel.

I, Caspar, follow this strange star
that shines and moves
as if its very motion declares
a coming moment in which we must attend.
Are we following or is it pulling us?
It curves close and near
as if it has secrets to tell.
I listen half-expecting it to speak,
for it knows more than we do.

I, Melchior, follow in fear
this poem of God
writ large with light.
How will we hear the unhearable?
How will we learn the unknowable?
Who am I to know such secrets?
Yet, the poem holds the very secrets
for which my soul yearns.
We hear a rumor of God come near,
stepping from behind his house of light.

I, Balthasar, walk in step with this star,
made in the earliest of days
when God clothed the void with light.
Now it leads us, a fire in the desert
blazing as in the old stories,
a lantern of God dazzling the sky
and shooting hope into our hearts.
We hear a rumor of a God who visits,
a God come near.